LC Not Listed

I0648551

Date

THE COMMUNICATION
OF THE GOSPEL

THE
COMMUNICATION
OF THE
GOSPEL

BY

DAVID H. C. READ

Chaplain to the University of Edinburgh

THE WARRACK LECTURES

FOR 1951

Mission House
Seminary Library

SCM PRESS LTD
56 BLOOMSBURY STREET
LONDON

TB4 9-30-58 1.33

First published 1952

Printed in Great Britain by
The Camelot Press Ltd., London and Southampton

WQ5
R22

To

THE PARISH MINISTER

Contents

Foreword

IT IS USUAL to introduce the Warrack Lectures on Preaching with a graceful bow to one's predecessors, and a modest reluctance to assume their chair. Such a gesture on my part goes without saying, and my only real excuse for following a series of Scottish ministers of mature experience and distinction of pulpit gifts is that I am in the lectures not dealing directly with the preparation and delivery of sermons. The question above all others that has seemed to me urgent for the Christian pulpit is the bridging of that expanding gulf between the thought and language of the inner Church and those of the contemporary world. And so I have attempted to make some assessment of the present conditions to which the Word must be addressed, and to draw some tentative conclusions for the preacher.

The students to whom these lectures were delivered in Glasgow and Aberdeen were a stimulating audience, and I hope that from them will come in future days a deeper and fuller answer to the problems I have raised than I was able to offer them. It will be obvious to the reader that I have drawn on the resources of many modern thinkers, British, American, and Continental—and not all theological. But perhaps I have been more aided by the friendship and discussion of a host of men and women whose names never appear in print. I am thinking of those in my parishes in Coldstream and Greenbank, Edinburgh; in Oflag VIIC and IX A/H Germany, and Edinburgh University; and in particular of the many friends who stand somewhere on the frontier of faith. It is to help the work of bringing the Christian Gospel into vital relationship with us all in the peculiar stresses of our age that these lectures were written.

I am grateful to the Revd. A. K. Walton, D.D., and the Committee on Education for the Ministry of the Church of Scotland for the encouragement of the invitation; and to the staff and students of Trinity College and Christ's College for their hospitality and warm welcome when the lectures were delivered.

And since I am convinced that the most important work for the Kingdom is being done in every land, and not least in Scotland, by the parish minister, who may never find time to read, far less to deliver, such disquisitions, I have taken the liberty of dedicating these lectures in their printed form to those who are thus serving in the front line.

DAVID H. C. READ

The University of Edinburgh

I

The Breakdown of Communication

A POPULAR FILM of the inter-war years had one little shot that has remained in my mind. It showed a preacher in action in his pulpit. He was an elderly man with a benevolent face and pleasant manner, and he was speaking on the relevance of the Christian faith to the national and international situation. What he was saying was true, adequately expressed, and of practical importance. Then the camera swung round and revealed a church containing two or three devout ladies at the front and a somnolent old gentleman at the back—and passed on to other matters. No comment.

The problem of communication for the Christian Church consists in reckoning with the somnolence of that gentleman and with the absence of his friends and relations. It is, of course a deeper question than the perennial 'Why don't people go to church?', but that picture may serve as a symbol of the major issue confronting the Church in the modern world—the lack of living contact between pulpit and pew, and between pulpit-and-pew and the world outside. It is not the content of the preacher's message that is the primary question to-day, nor even that of his method of delivery. It is the ever-widening gulf between the minority for whom the Christian Gospel is a vital and meaningful factor in their daily lives, and the great majority for whom it has little or no relevance at all. Those who are charged with the proclamation and expounding of the Gospel in this generation have got to reckon with this problem with open eyes before the Church becomes an isolated community speaking a different language and thinking other thoughts, while the world roars on to destruction.

We are dealing here with a universal factor in human relationships. Every creative encounter in society involves the mysterious trinity of thought, expression, and communication. We can observe this process in everyday conversation, but it is perhaps most easily illustrated from the world of art, for the artist is consciously and skilfully engaged in doing what everyone else is groping after all the time. The poet, the painter, the musician—and the preacher—have that within them which is ultimately indescribable but which for them is life itself. This original thought (for want of a better word) cannot remain private: it must find expression, and so the corresponding art forms—poem, painting, symphony, sermon—come into being. The process is vividly described from the point of view of the preacher in the words of Jeremiah: 'His word was in mine heart as a burning fire shut up in my bones, and I was weary with forbearing, and I could not stay.'[1] It is clear that the expression can never perfectly correspond to the thought, so the creative spirit must wrestle continually with the

[1] Jer. 20.9.

12

problem of incarnation in sounds, colours, and words. But beyond this expression, this incarnation, there is a further step—the communication to others. The thought may be real and deep, the expression adequate, but unless the spark of communication is lit nothing is conveyed, and the creative process is incomplete.

It is this trinity of human intercourse, with its remarkable analogy to the Christian apprehension of God as Father, Son, and Holy Spirit (so interestingly developed by Miss Dorothy Sayers in *The Mind of the Maker*), that is suffering a general breakdown. While our special concern is with the communication of the Christian Gospel it is right to see this particular breakdown as part of a much more general failure in communication in our civilization. The ability of men and women to understand one another, to commune, to share intimate experience, seems to have shrunk almost proportionately to the expansion of the physical means of communication. It is interesting to compare, for instance, Chaucer's pilgrims with their easy intercourse that transcended all barriers of class or occupation, as they jogged on their leisurely way to Canterbury, with T. S. Eliot's group of moderns in the Tube:

. . . when an underground train, in the tube, stops too long between stations
And the conversation rises and slowly fades into silence
And you see behind every face the mental emptiness deepen

13

Leaving only the growing terror of nothing to think about.

The artist, placed always at the sensitive point of society, is to-day reflecting in his own activity this widespread failure in communication. For it is not only the sermon that cannot sell. The modern poet makes probably less impact on the general public than in any previous age. The public retorts that it cannot understand what the poet (or the artist) is trying to say. The result has been that some writers and painters have been driven to make a virtue out of necessity and have declared that they are not interested in whether or not anyone understands what they are saying. It is difficult to believe that an entire subjectivism of this kind is consistent with the publication of books or the display of pictures, but it is evident that much of the imagery of modern poetry and art is of a semi-private nature, relying for the communication of the thought on the common stock of associations of a very limited number of people.

For the Christian preacher this threatened isolation is intolerable. The artist has a certain autonomy in his own sphere and can decide to whom and how far he is to be intelligible, but the preacher can make no reservations of this kind. If he is crying in the wilderness he can take no satisfaction from the sound of his own voice. It is for the wilderness that he exists. In other words he has no independent status whatever, but is simply a voice, a witness, and communication— not to his friends, or a spiritual *élite*, but to the mass of his contemporaries—is his sole function. His *raison d'être* has been simply and finally stated by St. Paul: 'Whosoever shall call upon the name of the Lord shall be saved. How then shall they call on him in whom they have not believed? and how shall they believe in him of whom they have not heard? and how shall they hear without a preacher?'[1] The preacher exists to communicate the name of the Lord on whom they must call to be saved. That means in modern terms that he must speak of the revelation of God in Christ so that the ordinary man can understand what it is that he is summoned to accept and believe.

This is what gives the question of communication its supreme importance for the Church to-day, and should make it a matter of serious thought for those preparing for the ministry. As preachers-in-training you receive in your theological classes the material for securing and extending your grasp on the Christian thought; in practical theology and in previous Warrack Lectures you have received excellent advice on Christian expression—sermon preparation, construction, and delivery. I have chosen to direct your attention specifically to the element of communication, for that seems to me to be the decisive point in Christian strategy to-day. We are not living in a period of great theological debate. Apart from the professional polemics of the theologians there is in non-Roman Christendom a most remarkable convergence of belief as to the fundamentals of the faith.

[1] Rom. 10.14.

This has been indicated not only in high-level ecumenical statements of faith, but in hundreds of conferences and missions where speakers are invited, and books displayed for sale, on the assumption that a wide variety of speakers and writers from different denominations will have roughly the same point of view. They will be fashionably—and I hope genuinely— orthodox as to the major items of the Christian creed. It would also be true to say that in modern preaching the Christian message is finding at least as careful and adequate expression as in any other age. If there are in this country to-day fewer 'star preachers' whose names will ensure a full church or hall anywhere, the average level of preaching, according to those more competent than I am to pronounce an opinion, is probably higher throughout Scotland to-day than at any time in the past. The absence of the 'star preacher' may, or may not, be a symptom of ecclesiastical health, but it is certainly a sign of declining popular interest in the affairs of the Church —in other words, of a failure in communication. It is, therefore, this problem that I want to consider with you—not primarily what is the content of our message as Christian preachers, nor the technique of expression, but the point of contact between the Gospel and the people, between the Church and the world. These lectures will be concerned, then, with preaching from the point of view of the receiving end, with the people to whom we speak.

When we raise the problem of communication

within the Christian Church to-day we are exposed to misconceptions, and in particular to two opposed heresies which seem to me to bedevil our thinking and planning.

In the first place, there is the tendency to believe that the problem of communication is largely a matter of technique, and that once we have found the right method of approach the world will respond and the Kingdom of God will have arrived. Psychological research, high-pressure advertising, opinion-polls, mass-suggestion, success-stories, modern business methods—these are the methods by which the masses are to be swept into the Christian fold. This is the Western heresy, for it is a reflection of the activism of an era of economic expansion. If we tend to associate it particularly with the United States to-day that is only because the vigour and enthusiasm of the American social climate exposes the churches there in an exceptional way to this temptation. But it is not a national so much as a regional and temperamental way of thinking. Wherever men are dazzled by the triumphs of organization and propaganda they will be inclined to put their money (both literally and metaphorically) on modern techniques as the solution of the problem of evangelism.

The danger for the Church lies in the subtle shift of emphasis from the objective truth of the Gospel to its pragmatic value to society. The Christian problem of communication is not to be solved merely by discerning what people want and giving them it. This is to transform the Gospel challenge of 'Repent and believe' into a cynical technique of winning friends and influencing people. The preacher who is sensitive to the public pulse at any given moment is always under the temptation of responding to a popular demand rather than demanding a popular response. In other words, he is eliciting, probably unconsciously, his message from those to whom he speaks, rather than witnessing to the truth of the entrusted message. I need hardly say that in discussing the problem of communication I have in mind that the preacher's first duty is not to offer the kind of pabulum for inner peace, poise and personality that might be more swiftly obtained by glandular injection, but to announce the good, but inevitably disturbing, news of God in Christ reconciling the world unto Himself.

In the second place, we have to consider a no less serious distortion of the New Testament attitude of an opposite kind. If the Western heresy vitiates the problem of communication by dissolving the message in a witches' brew of psychological techniques, uplift courses, card-indexes, and statistics, those who are loudest in their denunciation of this tendency often betray an equally dangerous misconception of the duty of evangelism. An unfortunate by-product of the theological revival of recent years is the growth of a totalitarian habit of mind which presents the Gospel in the form of a *Diktat*, and virtually ignores the condition of the hearers. We might call this the Continental heresy, for it is from our European neighbours that we have derived so much theological strength, and it is among them that an extremism can be found which amounts almost to a denunciation of all human effort to mediate the Gospel to our world. I remember once discussing with a group of theological students in Germany some modern experiments in evangelism, and finding among them a tendency to question the value of any kind of attempt to commend the Gospel to our generation, and to assume that any lack of popular response is due to *Verstocktheit*—obduracy, hardness of heart. They clearly suspected that much of our modern experimentation was based on the assumption that if only the right technique could be found the world would be bound to accept the Gospel, an assumption which they rightly judged to be foreign to the New Testament.

It is true that there is an 'offence' in the Gospel. But the answer to passivism of this kind is: 'Woe to him through whom the offence cometh!' The Gospel itself presents a moral challenge which not every man is willing to accept, but we are surely guilty if we add to this 'offence' stumbling-blocks of our own making. If we deliver sermons and addresses containing a faithful exposition of biblical truth and find that few will gather to listen and still fewer make any kind of response, it is only too easy to comfort ourselves with the reflection that the message is 'foolishness to them that perish', or that 'narrow is the way, and few there be that find it'. We ought instead to be asking ourselves if it is indeed the Word of God the people are rejecting, and not the irrelevance of the exposition, the ecclesiastical context, the obscurity of the language, or even the voice of the preacher. The Continental heresy

consists in such an emphasis on the orthodox exposition of the biblical message, 'whether they will hear
or whether they will forbear', as to involve an ignoring
of the condition of those to whom we speak. The
revival of Reformed theology, which I for one hold to
be one of the signs of hope in our era, has unfortunately
contributed to this kind of mis-interpretation; for it
has both developed a specialist terminology which all
too easily finds its way into the pulpit, and at the same
time encouraged the preacher to rely on the mere
proclamation of the word without much thought for
the response of the hearers. Put concretely, that means
that if you speak to a congregation about 'the biblical
paradox of man's radical sinfulness in the context of
redeeming grace', you must interpret the yawns in
the pew in terms of bewilderment of mind rather than
hardness of heart.

I trust that my references to America and Germany
will not lead anyone to suppose that in this country
we have followed a blissful middle path of successful
British compromise. We may, on the whole, have
avoided the extremes, but we have certainly not come
nearer to solving the problem of communication. It
might well be said that we have neither given ourselves
to the understanding of the Gospel with the passionate
intensity of our Continental friends, nor have we made
that contact with our generation on a broad front that
is typical of the best in American Church life to-day.
And probably the most promising signs of a new
power in Christian preaching are coming from those
quarters in the United States where the content of the

Gospel is being studied with a new seriousness, and from those quarters in Germany where attention *is* being drawn to the problem of communication. I am thinking, in the one case, of the influence on the younger generation of American preachers of such thinkers as Reinhold Niebuhr, John Mackay, Tillich, Trueblood, Mollegen; and, in the other, of the development in Germany of the laymen's movement and the new approach to the de-Christianized youth.

It might be helpful at this point to try to set the problem of communication for the Christian Church in this country to-day in as simple and concrete terms as possible, so that we can see what justification we have for putting it in the forefront of our thinking and planning.

I am going to ask you to imagine that you are that impossible person—an unbiased observer arriving here from some totally different civilization; if you like, a member of a mass-observation team from Mars. You would most certainly soon be struck by the immense network of churches, institutions and societies of a religious nature that covers the country. You would note that the vast mass of the population is within walking distance of a place of worship where at least two services are provided per week. Beyond this you would discover that the influence of the churches permeates the population through religious teaching in schools; Army, hospital, and industrial chaplaincies; social work, missions, campaigns, and a considerable allotment of radio time. You would find thousands of men and women devoted to the propagation of this religion in full-time employment, and probably millions part-time. You would of course be intensely eager to discover what message and way of life was being commended and furthered by this huge organization. And if you were skilful and shrewd enough to penetrate through the bewildering variety of expression in word and worship, and to ignore extreme deviations, you would eventually arrive at certain basic tenets which are being proclaimed or assumed.

We might summarize these tenets in some such way as this: (1) there is an invisible Deity who is ultimately responsible for the whole world in which we live; (2) human beings are designed to live in love and obedience to this God, and in harmony with one another; (3) God has made known His being and purpose for men supremely through the person of Jesus Christ, who is said to have lived in the early days of the Roman Empire, to have taught and practised the good life, to have been executed through the malevolence of His enemies, and to have appeared after death to His friends: (4) by coming into contact with this God through the still-living Christ men and women can be forgiven, learn the right path, and be given divine assistance to follow it; (5) these things are known to us through the books of the Bible and in the living tradition and experience of the community of Christ's followers from the beginning to the present day.

How would these beliefs strike you if you had never

heard them before? I think you would be inclined to make at least two observations: first, that these statements are of such practical importance for the business of living, and are so intrinsically astonishing, that they must evoke either enthusiastic belief or violent rejection, and, secondly, that, if these statements are true, they correspond in a remarkable way to what are apparently the deepest desires of modern man. He seeks a purpose: here is one offered. He wants some kind of guidance in the basic difficulties of life and death: here is an offer of light and power. He wants a sense of significance that reaches beyond this material world: here is a word assuring him of his eternal value. We should suppose, then, that this message, backed by such a huge organization and resources (such as would be the envy of any movement seeking to instil a new ideology into the masses), would be either totally rejected on the grounds that it is false, or else welcomed and practised on a nation-wide scale.

What, in fact, do we find? Here we have to make a big effort to detach ourselves from personal impressions and ecclesiastical pronouncements, and seek a dispassionate appraisal of the situation. There can be no doubt whatever that this Christian message has met with neither whole-hearted reception or rejection. The precise situation is perhaps impossible to tabulate, but recent impartial researches that have been made should give us food for thought.

It is reckoned that about ten per cent. of the population of Great Britain have a live connection with the

Christian Church. In Scotland the proportion may be somewhat higher, but a recent survey[1] states that half the population *never* goes to church, and indicates that of the remaining half only a minority is actively interested in the Church's work. The English community examined by Mass-Observation in 1947 showed some remarkable results in the realm of religious belief.[2] Only two-thirds of the men asked admitted to some kind of belief in God; forty-six per cent. of men and women were unbelievers or undecided as to whether there is any life after death; a quarter of those who go to church said they did not believe in the divinity of Christ. These figures may, or may not, represent the situation we know in Scotland, but we should be unwise to imagine that they are not fairly typical of the state of mind in the country as a whole. The general impression gained by impartial observers is well summed up in the *English Life and Leisure*[3] report which says that 'most people in Britain do not believe that the churches are relevant to life in the scientific age'.

There are few signs of an outright rejection of the Christian message. The Mass-Observation report was given the title *Puzzled People* because it became clear that there was no clear-cut trend away from traditional doctrines, but rather a strange, illogical mixture of

[1] *The Churches in Scotland To-day*, by John Highet (Jackson, 1950).

[2] *Puzzled People* (Gollancz, 1947).

[3] *English Life and Leisure*, by Seebohm Rowntree and J. R. Laver (Longmans, 1951).

belief, unbelief, half-belief, rationalism, and superstition. A man will say that he does not believe in God, and yet will admit to the occasional use of prayer; another who never attends church will profess belief in the divinity of Christ; another will confess to regular church-going, but deny the major articles in the Christian creed; and a great number of our contemporaries are revealed as strongly desiring that their children shall be taught in schools the religion in which they themselves have ceased to believe. All this goes to show that there has been no considered and explicit abandonment of the Christian message, and that no other religion or secularist philosophy has yet been operative on a wide scale to repudiate the traditional faith.

Most of us will have found, if we have moved sufficiently in circles outside Church membership, that this kind of confusion and doubt is reflected in many of our friends. The convinced anti-Christian is a rare phenomenon, but we meet hundreds who have the rudiments of Christian belief, yet little real conviction about God and the future life, and no confidence in the Church. We may preach sermons, or arrange lectures, to deal with just those points in Christian belief which seem most relevant to the situation, but the people who come to hear them are rarely those for whom they are designed. All this points to a breakdown in communication on a gigantic scale. The Gospel is being studied and proclaimed, the machinery of the Church is turning over with probably less inefficiency and wastage than ever before, but the religious state of the country shows that the bulk of the population is not responding with either acceptance or rejection, nor even showing any awareness that the message is relevant to their needs. It is evident that neither better arguments nor better organization will meet the situation.

Nor is it simply a question of finding new means of contact between the Church and the contemporary world. The problem remains in spite of our missions, invitations, commando campaigns, and radio penetration. We have to reckon with the breakdown within the Church itself. There is abundant evidence that those who attend worship, receive religious instruction, and share in the sacraments, are often also to be numbered among the 'puzzled people'. Any experienced minister will be able to tell you of the occasional shock he receives when a chance remark by one of his most faithful worshippers will reveal that some vital aspect of the Christian message on which he has dwelt again and again has completely failed to register. The surveys show that the bewilderment and uncertainties of our age are reflected as vividly inside the Church as outside. For instance, what are we to make of the report that of those who attend worship in a typical community, forty per cent. expressed disbelief in a future life? It is a tremendous temptation for the preacher, indoctrinated perhaps from his youth with the biblical faith, moving continually in circles where these things are taken for granted, and shielded by his collar from many of the expressions of everyday scepticism, and by misplaced courtesy from many of the honest opinions of his flock, to assume that the fundamental Christian doctrines are the unquestioned possession of his hearers, that communication has in fact taken place; while the true situation is that current scepticism and uncertainty have corroded the religious convictions of a high proportion of his congregation, and it is doubtful if more than a fraction of them could give to an outsider an intelligible outline of the Christian faith.

A message that is true and important, relevant and challenging; an organization of tremendous potential power; a people unconvinced, apathetic, puzzled. If that picture is accurate then it surely bears out the claim that the major problem confronting the Church to-day is not the content of the Gospel, nor the machinery of evangelism, but the point of contact between the message we know to be both true and relevant, and the people to whom for the most part it is only partly true and almost wholly irrelevant.

It is no use deluding ourselves with the comfortable words that historically these things have always been so, that from the beginning the Gospel was misunderstood and ignored, that in any age the bulk of mankind has passed by and the majority of the faithful have been relatively uninstructed. I have no desire to appear as a *laudator temporis acti*, still less to join the ranks of the defeatists, bewailers, and deplorers, who spread depression in the Church without causing a ripple outside. We may comfort ourselves if we like by the low ebb which church life has often before reached in this country. (When Sir Nicholas Bacon raised in the House of Commons the inquiry 'why the common people in this country universally come so seldom to Common Prayer and Divine Service' the date was 1572.) But the evidence is surely overwhelming, to any dispassionate observer, that the Christian Church to-day faces throughout the whole world a trend of thought, a social climate, a pattern of human behaviour, that is unique in its history; and that this pressure of our era has made the problem of the communication of the Gospel an urgent and major issue for all Christian people, and especially for those who are commissioned to preach. I am pleading here for a realistic appreciation of our lines of communication in the modern world, communication for a Gospel which I am persuaded has an authority and an appeal no whit less than when St Paul crossed into Europe. The next chapter will lead us to an examination of these factors in the modern situation which have produced what may fairly be termed the 'crisis in communication'.

II

The Pressures of Our Era

IF IT IS TRUE that we are faced to-day with a very serious breakdown in the lines of communication between the Christian Church and the world, then surely it is time that we devoted ourselves to a serious study of the factors that have contributed to this situation. The command to love God 'with all your mind' implies among other things an endeavour to understand the spirit of the age, and the command to love our neighbour involves the kind of sympathy that really *feels* the doubts and difficulties of our contemporaries, and the pressures under which they live.

Nothing does more to widen the gulf between the Church and the people outside than the withdrawal of Christians into the sanctuary where they can admire the colours of the stained-glass windows when they ought to be outside examining the dust that has blown upon them from the traffic on the great by-pass road. This is not a time to be exchanging glances of pious understanding in ecclesiastical corners, but to be out in the open exposed to all the winds that blow and trying the impossible of knowing whence they come and whither they go.

Let me warn you at this point that what I am going

to attempt here is precisely what you ought not to do in the pulpit. I believe it is our duty to attempt some diagnosis of the state of modern man, however inadequate it may be (and you have full liberty to disagree with mine), but the place to do it is in the quiet of our minds, by the fireside with our friends, or even, I am bold enough to believe, in a Warrack Lecture, but emphatically not the pulpit. Diagnosis is the endemic disease of modern preaching. You can hardly switch on a radio service without hearing someone dismally dissecting the body politic, or outlining the thought-processes of modern man. If you have a sermon that begins: 'This world is in a sorry state' I beseech you to burn it. In the first place, the average congregation does not really believe that the minister knows how the modern man thinks: in the second place, they get very tired of this 'modern man' and his near-relations, 'the man in the street', 'the average man', and 'the world to-day', and would willingly exchange the lot for a flesh-and-blood man or woman whom we really know: and in the third place, our chief task as preachers is to be announcers of good news, not midwives of calamity. In military terms, appreciation of the general situation is an essential preliminary for both strategy and tactics, but forms no part of the battle itself. A preacher indulging in diagnosis is like a general deep in appreciation of the total military situation when enemy tanks have already surrounded his headquarters.

Suppose, then, that for our purposes at the moment —in the training area—we do attempt an assessment of the situation. What are the typical pressures on modern man that have helped to make him impervious to the message of the churches?

The revolution in human life that characterizes our era, that has transformed, and is still transforming, the way men live and think, is surely that brought about by the dominion of the applied sciences—what is loosely known as technology. Everyone is aware of the outward manifestations of this revolution, the mechanical inventions of which our grandparents scarcely dreamed which are now part of the rhythm of everyday life. And everyone is also vaguely conscious of the acceleration in scientific discovery, the tremendous momentum of the penetration by experts into realms where the ordinary man cannot follow, but from which they may return at any moment with some fantastic new device for human weal or woe. But I doubt if we have yet fully taken account of the unique and catastrophic nature of the technological revolution in human history, nor of its repercussions in the human mind. We are still too deeply involved in it to assess its true nature: it would take a prophet of supersonic sensivity to discern the signs of our times. It may well be also that we are all of us in the grip of a fear that will not allow us to understand.

I know that in one way or another reference is continually being made in our pulpits to this situation. 'We live in an age of transition', we say, using a remark that was probably first made by Adam to Eve at the gates of Paradise. And the congregation sits back comfortably assured that this kind of thing has been said by preachers from that day to this. Or else we bombard them with 'crises', 'turning-points', 'dilemmas' and 'judgments', and then find that though our message has been appreciated, it has not been understood. Crisis-preaching simply comes up against the cushion of familiarity: we are the people who are paid to cry 'Wolf! wolf!' But perhaps we ourselves are not yet fully persuaded in our own minds. However important it is to express the sense of immediacy and crisis in our preaching, it is even more important to feel it in our bones, to be aware in the depths that we are really living through the most remarkable revolution in human history.

The real danger for the Church does not come from an overemphasis on crisis and judgment, but from the defensive reaction which says, in effect: 'Don't get excited, my boy. We've seen all this before. There have always been wars, and unrest, and atheism, and secularism, and revolutionary inventions, and the Church has come through them all. It's the same old problem of human sin we're dealing with.' That is the voice of delusive reassurance that tinkles through committees, and presbyteries, and assemblies, while the yogi and the commissar bend the course of history before our eyes. What is being said, in essence, is that we are not really faced with any new situation, that the changes of our day are only surface changes, more acute perhaps, but not different from the growing-pains of former generations. It is a tempting argument, but the facts are against it. And I hope that if you launch out to preach the Gospel in the conviction that we are living in a new and revolutionary world, you will not allow any of your elders, however wise and benevolent, to pour this warm water on your zeal.

Granted that no generation can form a just estimate of its own significance in human history; granted that we tend to dwell in youth on the revolutionary rather than the traditional in any situation; it is still, I believe, a matter of cold observation that the changes through which we are living are of such a kind as to make any theory of simple continuity in history absurd. The technological revolution began only some hundred and fifty years ago, just yesterday in the total human story; and, even so, it has not proceeded at a steady pace but rather with the acceleration of a geometric progression. Advances now happen in ten years which represent a more radical change than anything that took a century in days gone by. And this has been achieved by the phenomenal progress of the sciences and their rapid application to our living conditions. It is not surprising that our minds have failed to grasp the significance of what is happening, and that we tend to take refuge in the delusion that things remain fundamentally the same. (It is appropriate that the text: 'There is nothing new under the sun' occurs in Ecclesiastes, for it is a typically ecclesiastical response to the challenge of the new.) We hear, perhaps *ad nauseam*, of the failure of our moral progress to keep pace with the scientific, but there is an equally significant failure of our minds—including the scientific minds—to adjust themselves to the pace of new discoveries.

The outward effects of the technological revolution on the men and women of our day are obvious. The earliest, and one of the most spiritually significant, results of modern invention was, of course, the process of industrialization. The emergence of the industrial city with its agglomeration of men and women in the paradoxical combination of proximity and anonymity, was only very slowly recognized as a challenge to the existing pattern of Church life. The fact that the large industrial areas of modern Europe are now reckoned a target for evangelization similar to, and as urgent as, the pagan and Moslem worlds, is a measure of the insensitiveness of the Christian mind and conscience in the Church. We have yet to see whether, in view of more recent vast changes in man's life and thought, the message of the Church can be kept in touch with events: for in this generation we shall certainly not be granted the time to catch up.

What are some of the things that are happening under our eyes? There are some changes in the habits of mankind around us that are so evident we scarcely notice the revolutionary effect they are having on society.

Science has provided this generation with a whole range of instruments for reducing the time required for doing necessary work, and at the same time has offered another range of instruments for dealing with the spare time that has resulted. I make no apology for setting this question of man's leisure in the forefront, for the use he makes of his leisure is important in determining his character, and it is in his spare time, we must never forget, that a man normally listens to the Gospel. The man who listened to a sermon in Scotland two hundred years ago had little else to distract him. Gossip, a drink, an occasional book and more occasional newspaper (if he could read), perhaps some music and a game or two—that was the background, and not a dull background either, as we know from the memoirs, novels, and popular poems that have come down to us. But into such a leisure the sermon came to the common man as drama, as poetry, as material for debate, as well as the Word of God. His successor to-day is in a totally different situation.

Into the vacuum of his much greater leisure has come the mechanical entertainer and instructor. Press, radio, television, cinema—these account for such a huge proportion of his spare time that we are some-times left wondering what people did before they were invented. Compulsory education has made possible the simultaneous circulation of ideas through the popular press. A high proportion of the population is seeing the same films over a short space of time in their weekly or twice-weekly visits to the cinema. In a great number of homes, as your parish visitation will soon convince you, the radio is casting its pearls non-stop from morning till night. And soon the homes of the country will be subjected to another mass-pressure in the shape of television. These are not things to be cynical about, or to rage against. They are facts to be reckoned with.

We must realize that the mental background of our

potential listeners to-day is of a very different kind from that of their ancestors. They are exposed to a torrent of ideas among which they can rarely discriminate, and none of which has a reasonable chance to mature. (If we keep our sermons up to Third Programme level we must do so in the light of the fact that less than one per cent. of the listening population take that programme. The task of all Churches is to present the Gospel to men and women subject to these same stresses.) A sinister feature of the new situation is that our potential listeners have now become the targets of propaganda on a scale impossible in a previous age, with the double result that they unconsciously absorb much that is aimed at them, while at the same time they have become more suspicious of that which is obviously designed to sway their minds and hearts. Many of present-day values are derived from the cinema, and mass-entertainment is at work in the conditioning of men's minds every day of the week. These things affect all of us, but the academic training of a minister tends to make him think in terms of the one man who reads *The Times* rather the twenty that read the *Daily Mirror*.

Modern inventions of mass-communication, combined with compulsory education, have produced a type of person radically different in outlook, interests, and mental processes from those who lived from the Reformation down to Victorian times. The repercussions of this on our proclamation of the Gospel are surely considerable, and warrant a greater degree of study and understanding than has hitherto been given.

Forms of worship and of sermon have undoubtedly changed too, but have the changes been in any way commensurate with the change that has taken place in the minds and hearts of the people?

Another obvious outward pressure on modern man results from the extraordinary shrinkage of the world, in which no spot is now more than thirty hours flying distance from another, and no event of importance can happen anywhere without being known in almost every civilized country within a few minutes. I do not want to labour the obvious, but to draw your attention to some of the revolutionary effects of this shrinkage in the minds and habits of those to whom we speak in the name of Christ.

I spoke just now of changes coming over 'the human scene'. But a hundred years ago, even fifty years ago, there was really no 'human scene'. There was a British Empire scene, a Western European scene, a Far Eastern scene. Only visionaries and romantics could have used the expression 'one world'. But now men and women everywhere are sensing, even if they cannot articulate, the unity of the human family, and the interdependence of the nations. If the rise of nationalism in the sixteenth century was a revolutionary fact that had immense significance for the Church at that time, it is nonsense to suppose that this fantastic shrinkage going on before our eyes can be without meaning for the Church in our day. It has, of course, certain psychological implications which affect our preaching of the Gospel. We are speaking to men and women every Sunday whose heads and hearts have been badgered by news, usually of violence and catastrophe, which would never have reached their grandfathers at all, or else only with the cushioning effect of lapse of time. But surely more important is the divine opportunity that is afforded for the realization of the One Church of our Belief. For the paradox of world shrinkage is that the races and nations in being drawn together have not come to like one another the more. Instead, world-unification has raised national rivalries and nationalist passions to fever-heat, and only the reconciling Gospel of One Church can offer a solution. It is a solution that the world is more in a position to understand and to realize than ever before. Yet the ecumenical movement which God has raised up in answer to this need makes little progress. While the world races on to a unity of totalitarian domination, or a unity of dust and ashes, we find that in the same denomination in the same village St. Finnan's and the McFlannel Memorial cannot bring themselves to unite.

This problem of unity and peace, set us in acute form by modern means of communication, leads us directly to another tremendous pressure on modern man—the threat of scientific annihilation of body or soul, or both. It is true that the precarious nature of life in the twentieth century is really the normal state of man, a fact which was temporarily obscured in one small area of the world for some hundred and fifty years. (This was the period, incidentally, in which so many of our most popular hymns were composed.) But we cannot over-estimate the unique features of the present threat to civilization. Never before in human history has the actual obliteration of civilization, perhaps even the disintegration of the physical world itself, been within the range of possibility. And never before was it conceivable for one man, or group of men, to possess such means of control over the bodies and souls of others as to make possible the enslavement of the entire human race. These are facts which we have not really weighed. Perhaps they are still too new. But their subconscious effect on our world is already evident. I have the feeling that they are producing in modern man a kind of secular apocalypticism. We are now witnessing a curious reversal of rôles. Instead of the Church insisting on the realities of judgment and the end of the world to a population still peacefully dreaming of endless human progress, we are now beginning to find a secular world living under the perpetual shadow of annihilation, and a Church membership still on the whole indulging in the dreams from which the others have awakened. If the Church were really conscious of this pressure on men's lives our contemporaries would be offered more often and more vigorously the eschatological message of the New Testament, rather than the pious hope that if they are good we shall all return to July, 1914.

If, however, this secular apocalypticism might offer hopeful grounds for the preaching of an awakened Church, there are other pressures of the technological revolution that are not so congenial. In particular we have to reckon continually with the effect on men's minds of the very success of scientific discovery. So long as science seemed to be concerned with laboratory experiments, Boyle's Law, the movement of the stars, or theories of the atom, it was relegated in men's minds to the same category as the classics, history, or theology. But when science began to mean radio sets, vacuum-cleaners, penicillin, Mulberry harbours, atom bombs, then it acquired overnight a new and immense prestige. We can hardly over-estimate the way this has affected popular judgments, especially on such matters as morals and religion. The impression is widespread that science can do anything—and an omnicompetent Science that men could see in action seemed to have far better credentials than an omni-potent invisible God in whom they were asked to trust. No matter how many distinguished scientists publicly declare the limitations of their method, and renounce all claim to the discovery of ultimate truth, the general public still tends to believe that science has the sole key to human life and prosperity.

The pressure of this assumption will not be relieved by our constant stressing of 'spiritual values'; still less by any apologetic that tends to belittle the achieve-ments of modern science. (The preacher who hammers out an indictment of modern scientific inventions on a typewriter in a comfortable study heated and lit by electricity, and then proceeds by car to deliver it on the radio, is a warning symbol of a dishonesty to which we are all liable.) We have to accept the fact of scientific prestige and achievement, and try to cope with the illogical but powerful conclusions that are popularly derived from it. We shall not do this by harping upon man's inability to control the use made of scientific invention, or by dramatic references to the destructive forces that science has let loose upon the world. What we must recognize is that, for our contemporaries, the atom bomb is a fact, for good or ill, and as 'fact' is infinitely more effective and powerful in men's minds than the hell they once believed in.

'At the present time', says Jacques Ellul in *The Presence of the Kingdom*, 'the fact, whatever it is, the established fact, is the final reason, the criterion of truth. All that is a fact is justified, because it *is* a fact. People think that they have no right to judge a fact—all they have to do is to accept it. Thus from the moment that technics, the State, or production, are facts, we must worship them as facts, and we must try to adapt ourselves to them. This is the very heart of modern religion, the religion of established fact, the religion on which depend the lesser religions of the dollar, race, or the proletariat, which are only expressions of the great modern divinity, the Moloch of fact.'[1]

This is the habit of mind that we have to deal with, and it suggests that, unless or until it can be changed, the Christian message will have to be conveyed into men's minds on the wings of action and accomplishment.

The pressures created by the technological revolution—living in the mass; constant bombardment of ideas, news, entertainment; secular apocalypticism;

[1] *The Presence of the Kingdom*, by Jacques Ellul, p. 37 (S.C.M., 1951).

belief in, and fear of, the scientist—have resulted in a confusion of mind and paralysis of the moral sense on an unprecedented scale. Man is quite unable—we are quite unable—to adjust ourselves to conditions that are changing with bewildering speed. This has naturally led, among other things, to widespread nervous disorders whose incidence is most noticeable the nearer one comes to the centres of modern power. To this condition the Church can speak in the name of Christ the Healer—but only when we have felt on our own pulses the tempo of this distracted world, and have seen the Cross afresh as the sign of God's reaching to the depth of human despair. We have to remember that the widespread apathy of which not only the churches but nearly all organizations to-day complain is largely a defensive reaction against this nervous strain. A generation that 'has supped full of horrors' is on its guard against a really sensitive response to evil events. This is a totally different situation from that of Victorian Britain which was roused to fury by the news of Armenian massacres. Modern man can read of massacres, mass-deportation, torture and enslavement, without a twinge, and return unmoved to his football-pools. It cannot therefore be expected that he will be responsive to any sentimental appeal based on the sufferings of Christ. He must be convinced that Christ is one with him in his helplessness against evil, and that God was in Him reconciling the world unto Himself.

Alongside this contemporary indifference to causes and ideals we have to set modern man's notorious amoralism. In this country we are not yet faced with a rampant secularism that denies all moral values. The ideals of our Christian inheritance are still operative, if in shadowy form. But the confusion in men's minds, and the worship of scientific fact, has led to a moral scepticism, unconscious for the most part, but in the younger generation increasingly articulate. When Moody and Sankey conducted evangelistic campaigns they were speaking not only to people who knew their Bibles, but to men and women whose consciences were vividly aware of right and wrong. The modern evangelist is speaking to a generation which does not know its Bible and which has no moral certitudes. Logical positivism filters down from the philosophers to the average man who says: 'Don't know what you mean by sin: it's only a word.' We might well be surprised if we knew some of the quite fundamental doubts that arise in the minds of regular church-attenders as to the validity of our assumptions about good and evil, right and wrong. We are concerned with a world of eternal ends, of meaning, and of value: and on that assumption we proclaim our message. For many to whom we try to speak the world rather resembles a gigantic shaggy-dog story —one of these tales of a marvellously complicated machine which turns out to have no rational purpose at all.

It seems to me that the vital challenge to the Christian Church that emerges from these pressures of our revolutionary era concerns above all the reality and relevance of the Gospel. We are not faced with a generation of intellectual sceptics, or even of consistent materialists, but with bewildered, distracted, uncertain men and women, conditioned to respond to scientific demonstrations, suspicious of obvious propaganda, and unable to see much meaning in our religious propositions. Many of us will have had the experience of explaining the meaning of the Christian creed to an enquirer only to be met at the end with the plaintive remark: 'Yes, I can accept it all with my mind; but it doesn't mean anything to me: it's not real.'

It is idle to deny that this is a serious situation for the Christian Church, but I am not one of those who would bow to the storm, and advocate deep shelters for the Christian flock. If I have underlined what seem to me the catastrophic results of our revolutionary era, it is because I believe that we should go open-eyed into the battle. But those who believe in the Holy Spirit, 'the Lord and Giver of Life', know that His pressure upon our world is potentially greater than any other whatever, and that the recreative power of the Gospel is the only revolutionary force that refuses to capitulate before the 'facts'. To release this potential force God needs ambassadors of Christ who will be ready through toil and suffering to be really one with the 'puzzled people' to whom we speak.

III

The Involvement of the Church

A BOOK THAT has been almost forgotten in the last few years but which well repays our study is Adolf Hitler's *Mein Kampf.* Now that we can read it without the distorting sense of the living menace of the author hanging over us, we can learn a good deal from its turgid pages with their odd mixture of shrewdness, rhetoric, and prophetic power. The book certainly reveals very clearly that one of the secrets of the phenomenal, if ephemeral, success of the Nazi party was the Führer's skilful assessment of the moral and intellectual climate of his generation. However lunatic seems the philosophy behind it, however diabolic the practical consequences, the book shows a penetrating insight into the soul of the 'twenties, and a careful study of the contemporary European mind. Surely no less serious a study and assessment is required of us who are commissioned to preach, not blood and race and conquest, but the reconciling power of Christ.

There is a sense, however, in which this effort of understanding can deceive us as to the true nature of our problem, and entrench us more deeply than ever on the one side of the barrier between Church and people. We must remember the dangers inherent in a detached and intellectual approach to the problems of the age. While there is no doubt of the value to the preacher and the Church of a clear-headed, open-eyed assessment of the situation of modern man, even if we were able to carry this through with the utmost skill and insight it would be of little use for our evangelical purpose unless it were accompanied by a real sympathy —in the literal sense of 'feeling with'—with the world to which we speak. It is not enough to *know* the pressures of our era, we must feel them in our own blood. And to feel them means exposing ourselves, abandoning the illusory isolation of our spiritual fortress, and recognizing the true situation of the Church.

And what is the true situation of the Church? Surely not that of an observer, able to take a detached view of the modern scene and comment on it 'from above', as if somehow the Christian, and in particular the Christian minister, existed in a dust-proof case like the clock on a Victorian mantelpiece. Unfortunately, this is the impression all too often left on the world —the Church on the mantelpiece, remote, dustproof, and losing time. Sermons are apt to sound as if preachers were somehow preserved from the tensions and pressures that afflict their hearers. Time after time the familiar pattern emerges:—first, the diagnosis— the world to-day is suffering from this and that, the average man thinks so-and-so, modern science has given us, etc., etc.; then, the cure, the Christian answer, delivered in terms of guarded abstraction, unexceptionable sentiments but remote from the life of Monday-to-Saturday. 'O for the wings of a dove! Far, far away would I rove' is all too often the appropriate anthem before the sermon. And so the impression grows that the Church stands over against society, untouched by its agonies, immaculate in its irrelevant ideals.

The very fact that we are so prone to indulge in pulpit diagnosis betrays an unconscious assumption that we are detached observers of the contemporary scene. If we were where we ought to be—in the thick of the battle—we should not be so often in the position to make these assessments and generalizations. In P.O.W. camps during the war we spent a lot of time in diagnosing the war-situation. Contrary to popular belief we were extremely well-informed on current events; for we combed the German papers, heard their radio, heard the B.B.C. on secret sets, had first-hand accounts of actions from recent captives—and had hours of leisure to draw conclusions and form opinions. When an occasional airman from the thick of the battle was shot down near our camps and appeared like an angel from home, we invariably found that compared with the camp pundits he was almost totally ignorant of the war-situation. Might it not be that, if not more ignorance, certainly less utterance on the general world-situation might indicate a more serious commitment of the Church to the actual battle?

This observer-attitude betrays not only this academic remoteness but also a false conception of the relation of the Church to the world. We have been taught by modern apologetics to attack the myth of 'objectivity'

—that is, the claim of physical, political, or historical science to a totally unbiassed judgment of observed fact. It has been pointed out how the mind of the observer is inextricably involved in the process of investigation, and how his presuppositions, environment, and general *Weltanschaung*, are important factors in the operations even of the physical scientist. We must therefore be prepared to accept this principle in our own attitude as churchmen to the world— that we cannot be detached observers and critics as if the world were some extraneous object on which we could pass judgment. In our moral judgments, even in our declaration of the Word of God, we are not observers standing over against the situation, but are ourselves inextricably involved in it. We are commissioned with a word of judgment to our generation but we are not provided with a heavenly platform, suspended above the clouds, from which to declare it. And judgment, you will remember, begins at the House of God. We have a treasure that neither moth nor rust can corrupt, but we have it in 'earthen vessels' that are no more moth-proof or rust-proof than those of our neighbours. 'I pray', says Jesus Christ, 'not that thou shouldest take them out of the world', but that is just where we are continually tempted to imagine ourselves when we make our diagnosis of modern ills.

It is because the churches tend to forget their true situation in the world that they so often appear to our contemporaries in the rôle of a permanently-shocked and feebly-protesting grandmother. We know, of course, that this is a caricature, and that such an impression is fostered by the publicity inevitably given in the press to the more extreme expressions of ecclesiastical disapproval. But we should realize that the press carries such stories because they correspond to the ordinary man's picture of the Church as a body of people who are continually sitting in judgment on the morals and manners of the day. While I am not suggesting that the churches should abdicate their right to criticize, and if necessary condemn, modern social and moral trends in the name of God, I certainly believe that a more realistic identification of the Church, especially in its official aspects, with the men and women to whom she speaks, would lead to the sounding of a more positive note, and to a more ready audience for the message. It is, in the end, a valid and theological objection to some ecclesiastical pronouncements that they are 'out of this world'.

The attempt to maintain an attitude of remoteness from the world has blinded us to the extent to which the world and its pressures have silently invaded the Church. It is only by realizing our involvement that we can really be aware of the dangers of infection. To be in the world, but not of the world, is the almost impossible directive by which the Church must live; and there is a continuous penetration of the Church by the standards and values of the non-Christian world. I need hardly say that I am not referring to such social habits as were labelled 'worldly amusements' by an arbitrary piety which still survives to confuse the Christian mind. (As if there could be other amusements that are somehow 'other-worldly'). By the penetration of the world I mean the subtle and uncritical accommodation of the Church to the currents of contemporary thought and behaviour. It is always a difficult task to distinguish between the essential content of the Gospel and the words and ideas in which it is clothed; and between the essence of Christian worship and the social and cultural patterns in which it is expressed. This is to occupy us later: here I would simply draw your attention to the subtle way in which the prejudices and presuppositions of Western bourgeois society are interwoven in the fabric of our church life. A talk with a member of one of the younger churches of India or Africa, or with a Christian from behind the Iron Curtain, will very soon reveal to us the extent to which our church life has been moulded by the Western type of liberal democracy—as well, of course, as having moulded it. The trouble with this kind of pressure is that the inherent conservatism of ecclesiastical life makes the Church slow to reflect the changes in the cultural and economic pattern of society, so that its worldly clothes are never quite in the contemporary fashion. Can anyone doubt that the Protestant churches of Western Europe and America have on the whole tended to reflect the ethos of the dominant bourgeois society, and that, in this country at least, they have not even begun to reflect the transfer in political and economic power that is now taking place?

The specific modern pressures we were considering —the technological revolution, the scientific attitude, the dominance of means over ends—are also quite evidently being felt within the Church. It is not simply that the Church naturally attempts to use modern techniques and inventions and business methods for the propagation of the Gospel. That could with profit be done on a much greater scale, and we have much to learn from the United States in this connection. We have to be aware of something much more subtle that is continually active in the Church—the acceptance by Christians of the intrinsic value of activity for its own sake, the worship of success in terms of numbers and evident results, and the delusion that efficient organization is the equivalent of spiritual power. When we discover that the world is not interested in ultimate ends—heaven and hell, the Kingdom of God, growth into the stature of Christ—we succumb to the temptation of demonstrating our immediate results—our social work, our youth clubs, our special services, our startling conversions, our missions and campaigns, as if any of these was an end in itself. It is exactly the same type of pressure as is at work in the world that makes the Church liable to worship its machinery and bow down before the columns of statistics. At a committee meeting I attended recently, after an hour's vigorous talking a bombshell was dropped in the form of an innocent question: 'Just exactly what is the purpose of this committee?' Nothing is more disturbing to our concentration on means than the intrusion of the question of the end. What a breath of fresh air would blow through our churches if every committee, every meeting, every service were honestly to face this question of ultimate purpose. The advance of the Church in our age is surely impeded by the survival of a multitude of meetings, duly entered in our year-books, and counted to us for righteousness, which are attended out of a spirit of loyalty by good-natured people of whom it might be said as of the Ephesian mob: 'The more part know not wherefore they are come together.'

The emphasis on technics and practical results has also invaded the daily life of the minister. By all means let us have business methods in the Church. For too long in this country we have made a mental marriage of spirituality and inefficiency. But when we find ourselves too occupied with the card-index to talk to a human being in distress the time has come to resist the spirit of the age in the name of the Spirit of Christ. It is a salutary reflection that the reason why the priest and the Levite did not stop to help the wounded man on the Jericho road was not that they were hard-hearted hypocrites, but that they had an urgent appointment to attend the Committee for the Relief of Distressed Travellers. To keep our soul alive we must beware of capitulating to the modern supremacy of means over ends. Techniques of preaching, techniques of visiting, techniques of personal counselling—learn what you can from them, but hold them at arm's length, remembering the warning slogan of our friends in the medical profession faced with a similar threat: Operation successful: patient dead.

If, then, we are aware that we cannot be detached

spectators of the contemporary scene; and that the Church is perhaps to a greater extent than we think infected by the spirit of the age; how should we envisage the problem of the communication of the Gospel? Is there any principle in the New Testament by which we can steer our way in this complicated situation?

I believe that our situation is determined for us by the paradox of the Church being *in* the world but not *of* it. Christians are called to be the salt and light of the world, and neither salt nor light can operate unless they are on earth and not in heaven. On the other hand neither can they operate if they are so immersed in the world that the salt loses its savour and the light becomes darkness. 'I pray not that thou shouldest take them out of the world', says Jesus, 'but that thou shouldest keep them from the evil.' In the Book of Acts and the Epistles the paradox reappears in various forms—we are to love all men, but not to love the world that passeth away; we are to be subject to human authorities, but to obey God rather than man; we are to be ready to become all things to all men, but are not to be conformed unto this world. In a hundred ways we are shown the tension of the Christian life —a life utterly involved in this world, yet with its home-base in the world beyond. I believe that to-day we are summoned to take this paradox more seriously and to act on it more radically than at any time in the recent past. For it is not accidental, or theoretical, paradox: it is rooted in the supreme paradox from which our Gospel springs—that the Word was made

flesh and dwelt among us. The miracle of the Incarnation was precisely this linking of the apparently
incompatible. Jesus Christ was wholly in this world;
and wholly of God. In the life and preaching of the
Church we must be utterly and painfully *in* this visible
world; and yet uncompromisingly the witnesses of the
unseen God. The cross where God was in Christ
reconciling the world unto himself was planted in this
solid earth, and the Church that lives by that divine
event must be there too in the dust and the sweat and
the blood—in the world but not of the world.

The Church has always inclined to resolve this
paradox by neglecting one or other of the factors.
Fifty years ago the balance swung heavily towards
identifying the Church's aims with those of the
secular world, and eliminating the note of judgment.
Preachers exercized themselves in explaining away the
supernatural element in Christianity, and in accom-
modating the transcendent New Testament conception
of the Kingdom of God to the current myth of
evolutionary progress. We have to-day grown so
accustomed to reviling the optimism of the 'Rise-up-
O-men-of-God' period and exposing its too facile
wedding of Christian doctrine to secular hopes, that
we perhaps are failing to see how this tendency to
merge Christianity and current secular ideals persists.

To-day we are patently exposed to the danger of
identifying Christianity with the political aims of
Western democracy. It is not by any means always easy
to detect this process. We are all aware of the kind of
pressure a totalitarian system exerts upon the Christian

Church. We know, or by this time we ought to know, just how a Fascist or Communist government seeks to muzzle the Church and devitalize its message. The commissar who censors the sermons is at least a figure of flesh and blood whom we cannot fail to see. But in the much more congenial atmosphere of the non-Communist world we are much less likely to be aware of political pressure on the Church. The censors of our sermons are not sinister figures spotted by the beadle in the back row of the gallery, but the decent, good-hearted folk in the pews who are being conditioned to identify the political judgments of the Western world with the will of God, and who, probably quite unconsciously, expect us to provide spiritual ammunition for the cold war. It is a hard thing for the Church, fully realizing the threat of Communism to all that we hold dear, to perceive and resist the danger implicit in the call to be the spiritual wing of an anti-Communist crusade. We must ponder the judgment of Christians in Eastern Germany that it is easier to be the Church there among hostile powers than in the enervating climate of the West. Visitors from this country to the Kirchentag in Berlin in the summer of 1951 were strongly impressed by the depth and vigour of the Church life in Eastern Germany in face of an avowed enemy.

The main tendency, however, at the present time is probably not so much towards identifying the Church with power and policies of this world as in the other direction—that of resolving the paradox by attempting to remove the Church's real activity from the material world to some spiritual sphere. In our theological thinking we may have got beyond any crude division into spiritual and material, body and soul, but for many of our church-members the distinction is still accepted as almost self-evident. Thus while you must be prepared to hear and answer the perennial question: Why doesn't the Church give a lead? you must equally expect, if you do speak of Christian attitudes to politics, war, racial and social questions, that you will be asked: Why doesn't the Church mind its own business? And that question reveals the implicit belief of many good men and women that the Church's business is in some spiritual sphere quite remote from the world we live in.

Thus it is that we are expected to stand quite simply for the spiritual as contrasted with the material; and we tend to fortify this impression by indiscriminate attacks in our preaching on what we call 'materialism'. No one has yet been able to explain what this 'spirituality' is that can be divorced from the bodies it informs, the houses we live in, the food we eat, the economic life on which it depends, our relationships to others, and the political life that this involves. And certainly the Bible gives us no kind of a clue to such a barren spirituality, containing as it does so much more about politics, wars, economics, bodily health, food and drink, than about what the ordinary man calls 'religion'. Those who claim that the churches should occupy themselves solely with prayer and worship would probably be shocked to be told that this is orthodox Fascist and Communist doctrine. When

Hitler told Niemöller that the pastors could teach the German people about heaven and leave their earthly life to him he was simply putting in crude terms what many professing Christians imagine to be the true status of the Church. The Communists likewise are content to leave the churches to a spiritual vacuum where they minister to disembodied souls. The totalitarian leaders have had the intelligence to perceive that to isolate the Church from the material world is to make it an impotent and negligible factor in the affairs of mankind.

There is thus, in spite of the various ways in which the Church is caught up in the processes of the modern world, a strong pressure upon us to retreat from our responsibilities, and to deny our solidarity with the world for which Christ died. Even if we are aware of the falsity of the antithesis between spiritual and material, we may still be tempted to seek escape. For it is hard to accept our full involvement. The moment we seek to embody our Christian faith amid the ambiguities of our social and political life we shall certainly find trouble, and we shall surely make mistakes. It is easier to lead a prayer-meeting than to prepare a report for the 'Church and Nation Committee'. It is easier to preach on the sovereignty of God in glowing images and thrilling illustrations from ancient history, than to suggest its application to the contemporary scene. It is easier to devise a beautiful Remembrance Day service than to face the problems of the Church's attitude to war. I am not for a moment pleading for less emphasis on prayer, on doctrinal preaching, or on liturgical propriety. All these things need more attention than we give them. But I am suggesting that to take the Incarnation seriously, and the consequent involvement of the Church in the material world, means a continual wrestling with the concrete meaning of our prayers, our doctrines, and our devotions; and that this is a painful and difficult process that we are tempted to shun.

It seems to me that there are in the main two avenues of escape that we are tempted to employ. One means diving underground, and the other is to get on to the Mount of Transfiguration and stay there. Let me try to explain what I mean by these symbols.

First, there is a manifest trend in the Church to-day away from the problems of this world into the sphere of purely apocalyptic hope. This does not appear so much in our congregations perhaps as in the theological world; and is in any case more marked on the Continent than here. It rises from an utterly pessimistic judgment of the ways of the world, and involves abandoning all hope for this present age, short of the return of Christ in judgment. Again I am not deploring a return to a New Testament point of view in contrast with non-biblical philosophies of endless progress, but pleading that it be with the New Testament emphasis and application. For a belief in the coming of Christ, a conviction that He is the Alpha and Omega between whose comings our history is set in the Church, a realization of His ultimate judgment on all our policies and problems, can never be, on New Testament principles, a reason for evading or ignoring present social, national, or international problems. For the eschatological note of the Gospels and Epistles is always a summons to action and never a call to retreat from the human struggle and agony. Our duty is surely so to sound the note of Christ's kingship and judgment as to arouse our hearers to a new sense of their responsibilities in the world, and not to lead them to consign the world to the devil and sit with folded hands awaiting the millennium. When our contemporaries are everywhere only too ready to relapse into helplessness and fatalism, this is surely not the time for us to encourage a bolt down the eschatological rabbit-hole.

No serious Christian thinker to-day could deny the possibility of the Church being reduced to the position of a feeble, persecuted minority, unable to exercize any influence upon the powers of this world. In such a position she would inevitably be driven more and more to concentrate upon the one sure and certain hope. But we are not yet in that position, and it seems to me that some of our brethren are in altogether too much of a hurry to rush back to the catacombs. It is no wonder that the question is being asked: Does the Church offer any hope for this world, apart from the invitation to join a society which will be finally redeemed? What is our answer? I suggest that the parable of the talents has a precise application to this situation, for it was spoken, according to St. Luke, to those who wanted to go underground 'because they thought that the kingdom of God should immediately appear'. We are *in* the world, and it is there, enmeshed in its ambiguities, that we are to risk, to adventure, to gamble our lives in the light of the coming Lord.

The second trend away from our responsibilities I have called staying on the Mount of Transfiguration, for it means attempting to be the Church in glory while we are still the Church militant and struggling. The disciples, you remember, came down from the hill with Jesus, 'and much people met him'. And among these people we are introduced to a lunatic child, as a sign that we are again right down in this agonizing world. Peter had suggested staying on the mount—'Master, it is good for us to be here'—'not knowing what he said', for the place of the Church is not yet in the permanent glory of the Lord. To-day, the very crisis in communication tempts the Church to give up the attempt to be truly in the world, and to conceive of herself as already the immaculate Bride of Christ. Minority-consciousness can easily become spiritual pride, and one way of evading our involvement in the world is to conceive of the Church as placed above the sinning multitude, a remnant undefiled. No Protestant could dare to speak of a sinless Church, but there is perhaps a danger that we think in terms of the immaculate minority, standing beyond the crowd. While the Communist is committed to this heresy of an immaculate minority through which the world will be saved, the Christian knows of only one Immaculate, and must think of the Church as living by His power, but still immersed in this sinful world, and deeply involved in its desperate dilemmas.

For the Church is involved. By her nature and

commission, she is *in* the world as the redemptive community—not immaculate, not in glory, nor yet passively awaiting her Lord. The message we proclaim is of the reconciling of the world to God by the Incarnation of His Son, the Word made *flesh* (not spirit); His suffering in and with our humanity in the concrete realities of sin and suffering, sickness and anxiety, political intrigue, thirty pieces of silver, a crown of thorns, and a cross; His triumph over sin and death by His bodily resurrection; and His continuing work through His Spirit in His new Body, the Church. To proclaim this message faithfully means that our message is from above, and that 'here we have no continuing city'. But it means also realizing our position *in* the world: *we* are not from above, and this is the city that concerns us now.

The Church is involved—we are involved—for good or evil in every current of human thought, every activity of mankind. Our pulpits may sometimes rear up above the hearers like a heavenly throne, but we are not the men to speak from the height. It is our duty to be out and about in the world, hearing what others say, feeling what they feel, sharing their hopes and fears. Then as we sit to know what God would have us say to them, we shall not be thinking in terms of our appearance on a platform, orating from the height to the sinful masses below, but rather of what one sinner who knows something of the grace of God would say to another in all sympathy and sincerity as he sits alongside.

IV

The Word and the Words

A YOUNG MINISTER once described to me what he thought was the ideal building-plan for church and manse. I forget the details of the scheme, but the salient feature was a long straight corridor with a door at one end leading out of the manse study and a door at the other end opening into the pulpit of the church. Can you see the picture? The peaceful study—with the Bible on the desk in the centre, flanked by concordance and commentaries, the walls lined with the best theology, the telephone disconnected, and the door guarded by a zealous wife; and the other door (opened twice on Sundays) with its direct line to the pulpit, the highway for the Word of the Lord, the straight path from the mind of the preacher to the hearts of his hearers. No interruptions, no irrelevancies, no phone calls from Mrs. Brown, no last-minute intimations about next Thursday's social, no hawkers, no circulars—the preacher's paradise.

And what's wrong with this picture? Everything. That theologically-cushioned, isolated study is a lethal chamber, and it is a dead word that is carried out along the corridor. The sermon delivered at the other end—whether it flows over the somnolent heads of the congregation in a cascade of orthodox platitude, or whether it holds them spellbound by its brilliant originality and literary power—is not the living Word, spoken as it must be, from heart to heart and from life to life. The line of communication has been cut; and there is no real contact between pulpit and pew. Sad though it may sometimes seem to us in our dreams of the ideal sermon, conceived in quietness and delivered without complications, it remains an axiom of Christian preaching that the road from study to pulpit runs through a living, demanding, interrupting manse; out into the noisy street; in and out of houses and hospitals, farms and factories, buses, trains, cinemas; through ringing telephones and stacks of letters and minutes; up between rows of puzzled people to the place where you are called to preach. It cannot be otherwise. For the living Word there is no by-pass road from study to pulpit.

This necessity of a living contact with the real world arises both from our situation *in* the world that I have been trying to describe, and also from the very nature of the Word of God.

Our real situation is, as we have seen, not a spiritual isolation or moral segregation, but a full participation in the strains and stresses of our common humanity. To speak the message to our fellow-men we must be with them, among them, in living contact with as wide a variety of them as is humanly possible. In a book published twelve years ago I had the effrontery to open a chapter with these words: 'The trouble about clergymen, missionaries, and church-workers, is that they are always meeting clergymen, missionaries, and church-workers.' It was perhaps a judgment that the ink was scarcely dry on these words before the writer was whisked out of the ecclesiastical orbit and deposited for five years in the closest conceivable contact with stockbrokers, miners, engineers, actors, accountants, farmers, agnostics, atheists, fundamentalists, spiritualists, Moslems, Hindus, Jews—the whole cross-section that makes the British Commonwealth in arms. It was the best post-graduate school in practical theology that could be devised, although I heartily pray that you will never be enabled to enrol in such an institution. But thousands of others have made this same discovery in different ways—that a genuine, down-to-earth participation in non-clerical life provides the setting in which the Word can come alive.

I would not be misunderstood as suggesting that, in order to be in touch with our fellows, we should deliberately encourage additions to the multitude of calls and callers that surges around the modern manse, still less that we should abandon hope of securing time for uninterrupted study. What I would insist is that we never think of the demands of human beings as an irrelevance to our sermon preparation; and that we should seek, even at the expense of valuable time, human contacts well outside the circle of the church-minded. The clerical collar, which in itself I am neither commending nor despising, has unfortunately become a symbol of the *cordon sanitaire* that the world has drawn around the clergy. This is not to be dispelled by an artificial bonhomie, or a forced joviality; ('This merriment of parsons', said Dr. Johnson, 'is mighty offensive'); but by a genuine and wholly natural participation in the affairs and interests of the world we live in.

We must beware, however, of regarding this kind of participation as one more 'technique of evangelism'. We do not pass through the streets on the way from study to pulpit, self-consciously popping into this corner and that, in the pious hope that some stray acquaintance will follow us to church. It is through being what we are—men with like passions, struggling with daily problems, involved in the web of sin and circumstance like everyone else—that we are truly fulfilling our calling in the world as witnesses of Jesus Christ the Lord. For this living contact with men and women is implicit in the Word itself we are called upon to preach.

We must stop to consider for a moment what is the nature of this Word of God. It is not static, but dynamic. The Word is not a body of objective truth that can be mastered by the averagely-intelligent, and propagated by the competently-trained. It implies an encounter with the living God in which He assures us human beings, *as* human beings and not as intellects, or religious types, or a spiritual *élite*, that He is our Creator and Redeemer. We believe that the decisive action of God in this personal contact with men is Jesus Christ, crucified and risen. To proclaim the Word of God will thus mean bringing men face to face with Christ, and witnessing to a God who has conquered evil in love. At every stage we are dealing with a personal relationship, a living contact between God and the real world. The Word is not to be discovered in the study and delivered in the pulpit. It is spoken to us in the daily life of the human family, and spoken by us members of that family.

It is no accident that the Christian figure of speech for the communication of God to mankind is 'Word'. Other images of revelation used by religion and philosophy, such as 'fire' and 'light' have no necessarily personal implications. A word is a vehicle of personal communication, or it is simply an empty sound. The personal content of words can, of course, be so diluted that they become merely the means of conveying general information. When we read the directions on a tin of dried milk we do not feel in personal communion with anyone in particular. But the primary function of words is the imparting of self to another self. They convey, written or spoken, more than mere information. Man became a talking animal surely not just from the practical necessity of exchanging information, but from the desire to commune, to break out of isolation and fulfil himself in fellowship with others. It is this sense of personal communication that lies behind the biblical use of the expression 'Word of God'. While it implies at all stages an intellectual content—if you like, information about God—this is always subsidiary and contingent. That is why we can still find significance in the records preserved in the most primitive strata of the Old Testament, where the 'Word of the Lord' to Israel points to a personal relationship of communion, dependence, and trust, which is not dependent on the precise content of the message conveyed. (In our interpretation of the biblical 'Word' we are always, it seems to me, on safer ground even in the latest documents of the New Testament when we keep close to the strong Hebrew personalist thought rather than when chasing Greek notions of the *Logos* as a kind of impersonal reason.)

If, then, the expression 'Word of God' has this sense of personal confrontation, it implies a demand made upon man. Any real word spoken evokes a response. Our Gospel rests on the conviction that God has spoken, that He has taken the initiative in personal intercourse with man, and so the 'Word of God' lays a claim upon man. This is the typical biblical emphasis in contrast to the alternative conception of a 'vision of God'. We can experience a vision, be awe-struck by a vision, enjoy a vision—but it does not necessarily lay any demand upon us. It is worth noting that in one of the few occasions when we hear the word 'vision' in the New Testament it is in the curious phrase of St. Paul: 'I was not disobedient unto the heavenly vision.' A vision that one can obey or disobey is just another way of saying 'word'. A word heard demands some kind of an answer. We hear it, as it were, on our feet, ready to move. A vision we can enjoy on our bed and then turn round and go to sleep. When we read, 'My word shall not return unto me void', we know that the biblical view is that God communicates Himself effectively, and discloses His person, His real being, to men. Thus it is that, in the

Bible, the Word of God is always spoken in the context of real human experience: it is not a mystic event in the spiritual stratosphere. It is not really what we should call a 'religious' event in the sense of a Mahomet or a Mary Baker Eddy listening to heavenly voices, but something that happens right in the middle of everyday life. The Word of the Lord concerns personal relationships, social problems, national and international politics, and is heard in the concrete events of daily life. The living God makes Himself known to living persons, and they speak of him anthropomorphically and unashamed.

It is then entirely consistent with this understanding of God's personal disclosure that the fulfilment of the process of revelation is seen in His incarnation in Jesus Christ. That God can be known, and known as our God and Saviour, depends for us finally on the fact of Christ. This is above all else what we have to make known. 'God was in Christ reconciling the world unto himself . . . and hath committed unto us the word of reconciliation.' Before we can preach, before we can communicate anything at all to our generation, this is the fact that has to lay hold of us, the one central miracle on which our faith depends—that the Almighty God, in order to bring men and women into a personal harmony with Himself, and with one another, took our nature and in Christ exposed Himself to the entire range of human experience, meeting evil in all its forms, and accepting the utmost it could do. 'The Word was made flesh, *and dwelt among us.*' This is the involvement of which we were thinking.

In a human body like ours He was involved in this world. If the Church is involved to-day it is because she is still His Body. He was flesh and blood, like us. He spoke the words of a human tongue; He was exposed to all the pressures of His day. Our Gospel is not based upon an idea, an inspiration, a blessed thought. Our Word is not of an escape to another world. He dwelt among us. We speak of something that happened, an historical event in space and time, that conveys to us, and to all who will hear, the assurance of the living God who forgives, and restores, and empowers.

Unless we ourselves have heard this Word, not as a religious theory, not as a theological text-book, not as traditional piety, but as Real Presence, and are utterly persuaded that it is good news for all mankind, then we need not trouble about the problem of communication: for we have nothing to communicate. Our concern as a Church with the methods of evangelism, the points of contact with our generation, would be just another example of the modern worship of 'means' for their own sake. In my concern in these lectures with the outward movement of the Church upon the Word I am trying never to forget that inward movement whereby the Church at worship hears and re-hears the decisive Word spoken in the events of Christmas, Good Friday, and Easter.

But now we must ask: How is it that these events convey anything to us at all? If we can understand in any way how some things that happened in a corner of history have brought to us a conviction of the active presence of the living God, then it may help us to convey this Word to our world of puzzled people.

The answer to the question: How did I come to believe the Good News? cannot be given in simple terms, but there is one unescapable common factor in the experience of every Christian. We have been brought into touch with the community that has preserved the record of the facts, realizes their significance, and in one way or another lives by them. In other words, we know of the Word of God to us because in our own situation we have heard the words of the Church, mediated to us by parents, teachers, ministers, and friends of all ages. We can never get away from the contingency of birth. 'We are Christians', says Montaigne, with disconcerting finality, 'by the same title as we are natives of Périgord or Germany.' The presence of the Church is in this sense the condition of communication, and the extension of the Church into areas where the Gospel has not been heard, and the revival of the Church in the fossilized sectors of Christendom, are the obvious first steps of evangelism in our generation.

The words of the Church, however, are human words, subject to all the distortion and ambiguity of our speech. There is no other way in which the Word of the living God can be conveyed to men. Just as the Word Incarnate was exposed to hunger and thirst, weariness and pain, so the Church's words go out unprotected into the storm. As preachers we must accept this 'foolishness'. There is no possibility of finding an infallible formula, for we are not dealing

in magic but with God's relationship to His children
in the superb and tragic mystery of their freedom.
How then can we find these words meaningful in
our present situation, and powerful to convey the
Word of God?

In the first place, it is only if they *are* modern words
that they can be the Word of God to this generation.
If we were to read the Gospel in the original Greek to
a congregation the divine Word could not possibly
have entrance. We must remember that it follows that
if we speak the King's English and our hearers say it
was all 'Greek to them' the same judgment falls. A
great deal of modern preaching that is quite faithful
to the transmitted Gospel fails to become the Word
of God to the people just because it is not modern
enough. Modernity in this sense has nothing to do
with eliminating the 'scandal of the cross', but everything to do with eliminating the scandal of archaic
expression. The first written words in which the
Word was clothed were not elegant phrases of classical
Greek but the rough vernacular of the Graeco-Roman
world. If the Church of the twentieth century is bound
in its utterance by the cadences of seventeenth-
century prose and nineteenth-century poetry it is not
surprising that it is an opaque medium for the Word
of God. When you and I first came to know the living
God within the Christian community it was through
words that were familiar, the phrases of everyday.
It is here that the practical importance for our preaching of that living contact with the ordinary world
is most clearly seen. For there is nothing that more

effectively cuts communication with our hearers than a remoteness of language and archaism of style.

I am not recommending that we should stud our sermons with slang, or mould them to the shape of a leader in the 'Daily Express'; but we should do well to study some of the methods of modern journalism. For preaching is more akin to good journalism than to the literary essay. And even if we avoid the latest slang in our sermons we ought at least to be sufficiently aware of it to avoid minor catastrophes. (I heard recently of a saintly minister and excellent preacher who was delivering a wedding address to a young couple whom he knew. The closing words of a moving sermon were: 'And now, my dear young friends, if you have come to the House of God seeking His blessing on your new life together, you have had it'!)

This, then, is one requisite of the preaching of the living word in our generation—that it should be in the words of this generation and not of the one before; that it should arise out of our genuine participation in the life of the modern world.

If we now ask: In what way is this modern expression related to the saving events, the divine intervention in Jesus Christ? We must consider what it is in the life of the Church that prevents the distortion of the message. For it is clear that there is no outward guarantee that modern words will continue to represent the Word spoken by the apostles.

In the Reformed Church we neither claim nor desire to have an infallible instrument for defining the dogma that shall be preached. We can attach no sacro-sanctity to any form of words expressing the Gospel of the Word made flesh. The living Word that is sharper than a two-edged sword can cut through any formula or pattern of words. 'Languages', said Luther, 'are the sheaths in which the sword of the Spirit are placed', and sheaths wear out. If the Word of God is a living contact between man and his Lord it cannot also be a deposit lodged in some ecclesiastical bank. At the same time we are not thrown back on a purely subjective impression of what the message is about. There are at least three factors operative in the Church which keep the words of preaching in constant contact with the Word spoken in Jesus Christ.

(1) Wherever the Church exists the words of preaching are, or ought to be, accompanied by the celebration of the sacraments. Calvin was not merely being traditional when he linked the Word and sacrament as marks of the true Church. For the two are ultimately inseparable. The use of words in preaching is itself a sacramental action, for words are human instruments through which, by grace through faith, the divine Word comes. And the sacraments are, like preaching, a vehicle for the Word, the living contact between God and man in Christ. But baptism and the Lord's Supper proclaim this Word in another medium. And that medium—the sensible signs of water, bread, and wine —has a constancy that is denied to human speech. The actions of baptism and Holy Communion, when closely allied to the preaching of the Word, thus serve to keep the latter from drifting away from the decisive acts of God in Jesus Christ. Every minister of the

Gospel knows how, when preaching at the sacrament of the Lord's Supper, he is irresistibly drawn to declare the central facts of the Gospel message.

(2) In considering the relationship of our preaching words to the events in which God was in Christ reconciling the world unto Himself we cannot miss the decisive significance of the Scriptures. As the written record of the men who were nearest in time to the events that culminated in the Word becoming flesh they are the controlling factor in all our preaching. In them we hear the Word of God at the turning-point of human history. If we want to know how God has personally disclosed Himself to mankind we turn to the witness of prophet and apostle. We have, in particular, no other access to the facts concerning Jesus of Nazareth than this testimony of those 'who heard, who saw with their eyes, whose hands handled the Word of life'; and any claim to go behind these documents to find another Jesus is impossible. We may discuss various readings, incline to this interpretation rather than that, argue about one or two books on the fringe of the Canon, but in its steady central witness to the actions of the living God in our history the Bible remains the norm for Christian preaching.

To be faithful to the Bible in our communication means therefore that we are truly speaking about the saving facts the world must hear. That is why a text, and not a pretext, should normally introduce our sermons; and why expository preaching should be the rule in the Christian Church. But we must not forget that being faithful to the Bible also means finding the words of the present-day for the message we discover in its pages. For the Bible itself is an example of the living Word clothed in contemporary words, and our task is, if not exactly to build Jerusalem in England's green and pleasant land, at any rate to labour over the construction of a modern framework for the Word rather than to offer our contemporaries a pre-fabricated biblical model. We must remember that our age has not a strong historical sense, and that one of the blunting factors in modern preaching is the impression we too often give of dealing with 'old, unhappy, far-off things and battles long ago'. Biblical preaching gives us the pre-requisite of communication—vital contact with the Word spoken in Christ; but it ought also to imply a clothing of that Word in concrete modern terms. Beware if expository preaching seems easy.

(3) Preaching in contemporary words, based on the Bible, accompanied by the sacramental life of the Church, would seem to be the means whereby the living God has spoken to us through His Son, and therefore the means whereby He can communicate with the modern world. There is, however, something more to say about the relationship between the Word and our words. For we must ask: How is it that a man to-day, hearing another speak, or reading what another has written, really knows that God is addressing him? How is it that we can hear the Word of God Himself through the words of an apostle or prophet written in a context and idiom foreign to our own? How is it that the Church experiences the living

presence of Christ in the sacrament of the Lord's Supper? Not one of these things can happen to order: yet they *do* happen. Communication, thank God, does take place. The reconciling love of God is made known to our generation as powerfully as to any people in the past, in spite of our problems of communication.

The only answer to these questions is—the action of the Holy Spirit. The reason why in these lectures I have not before spoken of the Holy Spirit is simply that too often an emphasis on the work of the Spirit is used to foreclose discussion on the question of communication, and to avoid our responsibilities. The old saying is applicable here, that the Christian's duty is to work as though everything depended on us, and to pray as though everything depended on God. To say that ultimately the communication of the Gospel is the work of the Holy Spirit is the right of those who are prepared to strain every nerve to understand our age, to enter into it and be thoroughly involved, to wrestle with the words in which the Word is clothed. On the lips of those who are content with some traditional pattern of piety or ecclesiastical order, it is a soporific platitude.

At the beginning of these lectures I spoke of the trinity of thought, expression, and communication in all human intercourse, and remarked in passing on its analogy to the doctrine of the triune God. Whatever theological basis there may be for such an analogy I am sure that in the Bible the Holy Spirit represents God in active communication with the human family.

He is the Lord and Giver of life, the one who makes the divine thought and its expression real, living, and contemporaneous. He comes upon a group of men and women at Pentecost, and a Church is born realizing the living presence of Christ. He touches a human heart to-day, and a man or woman is awake to God. He takes a piece of Jewish history, a recorded word of Jesus, an argument of St. Paul, and God speaks directly through them. He comes upon the bread and wine, and the worshipper is united with the living Christ. Always and everywhere He is the Contemporizer, the Communicator. The real connection between the Word of God made flesh in Jesus Christ and these fumbling words of ours is the Holy Spirit of God who makes the dead bones live.

When, therefore, we have been in the study with the Bible, the commentaries, the dictionary; when we have gone out along the only path to the pulpit— the one that leads through the noise and strain of the modern world; when we find ourselves among the puzzled people, thinking with them, feeling with them; then, and then only, can we pray with the whole Christian Church: Come Holy Spirit. . . . For to have heard the Word in and through the words of the twentieth century, to be familiar with prophet and apostle and with journalist and technician, is to prepare the way along which our God can come.

V

The Pattern of Preaching

THE LIFE OF the Church in every age has an inward and an outward movement. The inward movement is the offering of worship to God, which includes the receiving of the grace of our Lord Jesus Christ, responding to the love of the Father, and experiencing the fellowship of the Holy Spirit. The outward movement is the witness to the world, the making known of the Good News, with the object of bringing others into the fellowship in obedience to Christ the Lord. This rhythm of worship and evangelism determines every aspect of the Church's life, and should be reflected in every member of the Body. Owing to the diversity of gifts in the Church, which is normal— owing, also, to our present mania for specialization, which is abnormal—we tend to overlook the necessity for every member to be engaged in this double movement. Thus we are only beginning to recover the belief in the missionary function of every lay member, and the use of the local congregation rather than an outstanding personality as evangelist. It is taking a long time to instil the understanding that the obligation of ordinary church membership is not only to attend worship and support the Church's work, but actually to communicate the Gospel. In the same way we are in constant danger of forgetting that the preacher is not simply a man called to proclaim the Gospel and to lead in worship—but to be himself a worshipper.

In our consideration of the problem of communication in the modern world, which is in a special sense the problem of the preacher, we must keep in mind the necessity of his sharing in this inward movement. It is not the purpose of these lectures, nor within the powers of the lecturer, to speak adequately of the devotional life of the minister of the Gospel; but perhaps I might quote these impressive words of Gregory the Great:

> True preachers both aspire in contemplation to the Holy Head of the Church, that is the Lord, above; they also descend in commiseration downwards towards his members . . . within they consider the secret things of God; without they carry the burdens of the worldly. . . . Love rises wonderfully to high things when it is compassionately drawn to the lowliness of its neighbours; and the more kindly it descends to the weak things of the world, the more vigorously it recurs to the things on high. . . . The pastor should not relax his care for the things that are within, in his occupation among the things that are without; nor yet neglect to provide for the things that are without, through his absorption in the things that are within.

Keeping this picture in our minds of the preacher's true participation in the rhythm of the Church's life, we must return again to the question of the significance of his special function in the modern world. For the place of preaching in the Church's strategy of communication is being seriously questioned. Things have changed since the days of Gregory, or Luther, or Knox, or Chalmers, or Spurgeon. The factors that we have been considering in our appreciation of the modern situation suggest a serious deterioration in the power of the spoken word to persuade mankind to accept the Gospel. The mass of printed material and the capacity to read it; the filling of leisure to saturation-point with mechanical means of amusement; the impact on men's minds of a stream of news from every part of the world; the growing suspicion of ideological propaganda—all combine to lessen the importance of preaching as a social phenomenon, and to lower its prestige in the popular mind. The most powerful sermon to-day has to compete with forces utterly unknown to our predecessors for the possession of men's minds and hearts.

In face of this situation there has been a tendency in the Church to discount the preacher's function in the life of the Church. Some draw our attention to the fact that the main trouble is not the inaudibility of the speaker but the invisibility of the audience, and draw the conclusion that the real centre of Christian witness to-day is not the pulpit but the homes and clubs and factories where the Christian layman is in touch with the pagan world. Others would claim that the line of communication to modern man is more visual and emotional than auditory and intellectual, and that therefore we should rely upon pageantry, dramatic ritual, films, and a rich and moving form of worship, to convey the Christian message. Others would take an even stronger line and say that the Christian pulpit should fall silent until the Church shows itself a practical force to be reckoned with in the body politic.

There is force behind many of these arguments. We must accept the fact that the pulpit cannot have the same status in society as it had in a less complicated world. It is perfectly true that the evangelistic task to-day cannot possibly be overtaken by the professional preacher, and that to an increasing extent we must rely on the layman at the frontier rather than the clergy in their citadel. And, in Scotland at least, we need to be delivered from an intellectualism that has been the besetting vice of our worship, and to realize the value of colour, movement, and drama as servants of the Word. We must also, I think, admit that there is a disproportion between our incessant idealistic language and the results the world can see.

In spite of these considerations I believe that not only does preaching remain a primary function of the Church, but that it can still be a real force in the modern world. The Oxford Dictionary defines preaching as 'to proclaim by public discourse', and so long as we understand it primarily as a proclamation of the Gospel it must remain central in the Church's life. It is significant that no church which neglects the pulpit has retained for long a living contact with the community. The general habit of judging a service by the quality of the sermon may be entirely wrong-headed, but it is symptomatic of a deep desire to hear something spiritually real, intellectually respectable, and emotionally satisfying. To clothe the Word of God in modern words of this kind is a demanding task that we have no right to shirk. Unfortunately the Oxford Dictionary has another definition of preaching which reads: 'to give moral or religious advice in an obtrusive or tiresome way'; and where that is the dominant impression we might as well banish the sermon for good. It is only as servants of the Word that we have a right to intrude our voices on the worshipping people.

Again, it is by no means certain that the spoken word has lost its influence in this mechanized world, in spite of its mighty competitors. Quite apart from the fact that it has wrested a new power from science itself in the form of radio diffusion, it is still a force in its own right for directing the minds of men and swaying the policies of nations. The Nazi party which came within an ace of conquering Europe and determining the lives of generations was borne to power on the spoken words of Hitler and Goebbels; and to-day the passionate speech, the reasoned argument, the dynamic utterance, are playing their part in all kinds of groups from monster rallies to selective cells at all the sensitive points of the international scene. It is inconceivable that the Christian Church should lose faith in this instrument of evangelism at such a time as this, when the seven devils are talking themselves into the vacuum of the human soul. There is, of course, particularly in this country, a deep suspicion of oratory —based on the quite unfair assumption that if a man goes to great trouble in the preparation and delivery of what he has to say he must therefore be insincere— but the British public can still be powerfully swayed by the spoken word, in fact by the oratory it does not recognize as such. No mechanical instrument has yet effaced the influence of facts and ideas conveyed through personality, the personality of a public speaker. The radio, which has so immensely enhanced the power of public speech and makes possible the swaying of a hundred million minds at once, abstracts from the personality the power of physical presence and gesture; but just as the microscope reveals the hidden constituents of the human body, so the microphone detects the sincerity of the human spirit. And so the old definition of preaching as 'truth through personality' gains relevance in a new medium. The advent of television, which at first seems more favourable to a ministry of action and ritual than of the Word, nevertheless opens out new, and as yet scarcely explored, possibilities for the proclamation of the Gospel.

If the Christian Church is to be really in touch with this mid-twentieth century, if our proclamation is to be effective, we shall need to reconsider the accepted pattern of preaching. I have no immediate startling suggestions to make as to what we must do, but it is surely evident that the preaching methods of to-day, like the rest of the Church's life, have not kept pace with the tremendous changes we have noted in the human mind and heart. It is hard to realize vividly the fact that preaching is fundamentally the use of words to convey the Word of God, and that there is no divine sanction whatever for the way in which this may be done. There is no form laid down, no Warrack Law, no commandment to say that it shall be done at 11.30 a.m. and 7 p.m.; no biblical injunction that it shall last twenty minutes (just the warning that when St. Paul went on too long, Eutychus fell out of the window). It is unwise, of course, to imagine that you are called upon to make revolutionary changes Sunday by Sunday—especially if it happens to be your first change. There is accumulated wisdom in most of the forms that have come to be accepted. And you will find that the average congregation is much more conservative than their minister in the matter of ecclesiastical experiment. That brings me to the first of the points I want to make in considering the general pattern of preaching.

The time is surely upon us when we need to draw a clear distinction between two classes of people to whom we speak. In the earliest days of the Church this distinction was evidently operative. In the New Testament itself we find that St. Paul in the Epistle to the Romans, parts of which at least I assume to be preaching material, adopts a very different method and vocabulary from those he uses, for instance, in the reported sermons in the Book of Acts. The distinction seems to have been preserved by the Early Church in the separate provision made for the faithful and the catechumens, and the contrasted methods of the instruction within the Church and the *Kerugma* of the market-place. Such differentiation naturally became blurred when the Church moved into the Constantinian period, and extinguished when 'Christendom' became an accepted fact. For centuries in this country the preacher could at least assume that the vocabulary and ideas he used in the pulpit were more or less public property. To-day we can make no such assumption, and are clearly edging back nearer to the position of the primitive Church. We can speak to the live inner core of our churches, whose religious and moral insights correspond roughly to our own, and to whom biblical words and imagery are familiar; or we can speak to the majority in whom the pressures of the modern world have nearly obliterated traditional moral and religious values, and who are theologically and biblically illiterate. It is becoming increasingly difficult to do both at once.

There is a faint recognition of this distinction in the old Scottish custom of addressing the 'saints' in the morning, and the 'sinners' at night; and it is perhaps a safe rule to have chiefly in mind at the morning service the committed Christians who are looking for something stronger than milk. But we shall have to bend our minds far more seriously to the problem of speaking to the man in the street, who is only sometimes, or never, in the pew. It is in this kind of proclamation that we are failing so miserably. We have now reached a stage when the kind of sermon that is acclaimed by the church-minded as a masterpiece of exposition, or a most inspiring and moving appeal, passes right over the head of the stray pagan as a succession of meaningless noises. It is, of course, the radio that reaches the mass of those who are out of touch with the churches, and the reaction of listeners to religious broadcasts is significant on this point. A conventional service with a good traditional sermon will bring enthusiastic letters from within the inner circle of the Church—and silence beyond. An experimental service, or unconventional presentation of the Word, will elicit appreciative comment from the non-Church world, and some indignant, and even rude, protest from within the Church.

Now it seems to me quite essential that in some of our Sunday services, in all our evangelism, and in nearly all our broadcasting, we should have in mind these people for whom Genesis is a biological term and Revelation the name of a suitcase—in other words the millions of our contemporaries who have not got to the starting-line of theological thought, for whom it is not only our use of terms like 'salvation' and 'adoration' that are meaningless, but often the very word 'God' itself. If we keep them in mind in establishing the pattern of our preaching, provided we do not neglect the needs of convinced Christians, we shall probably find that we are hitting the mark more often than we think.

There are, as we have seen, certain constant factors in all Christian preaching. It involves, to put it as briefly as possible, contact with the Word and contact with the world in the context of the Church. I want to say something about each of these in the light of the critical 'missionary situation' of the Church to-day.

(1) By contact with the Word I mean the living conviction of the preacher that God has spoken to him and to all mankind through Jesus Christ His Son. The very writing of that sentence reminds me that this is precisely the kind of statement that leaves many of my friends either full of questions or without a clue. Nevertheless within the Church we know what we mean by such words, even although there might be slight differences in interpretation. And the conviction that we express by these words is the foundation-rock of Christian preaching. We must guard against the possibility of explaining, and interpreting and re-interpreting till we are left saying nothing at all. It may well be that there are certain words and expressions that are opaque to the average man and yet are at present essential to the preservation of the Gospel. We have no right to suppose that the challenge of the Gospel can be wrapped up in words of one syllable so that the most casual passer-by will be compelled to stop and accept it. We are assured that the kingdom of God is open to the child, and the child-like mind, but not that it has a wide-open door flood-lit for the careless and indifferent. In all our discussions about communication I am haunted by the refrain of Jesus: 'He that hath ears to hear, let him hear'; and His enigmatic use of the parables 'that seeing they may see and not perceive'.

Contact with the Word Incarnate through the Holy Spirit active in worship, prayer, and sacrament means that it is Christ Himself who can speak through us.

In the first pulpit I entered as a probationer my eye caught a small brass plate with the words inscribed: 'Sirs, we would see Jesus', and no one can see Him in our words unless we have been with Him. That is the centre of the pattern of our preaching. Contact with the Word that comes to us in Scripture means that our words and imaginations are controlled by the given facts of the Christian Gospel. However much we may envy an official of the B.B.C. his magnificent title of 'Director of the Spoken Word' we must accept our position as 'Servants of the Entrusted Word'. It is always possible to select from the Christian tradition religious truths, or half-truths, that are acceptable to the modern man and innocuous to his pride. Probably most of us who have attempted to talk the language of the unbeliever have been guilty at times of such selection. For to go too far in talking his language is to risk ending up by thinking like him too. There is a hard core in the Christian message that cannot be whittled away by linguistic tricks, or dissolved in popular sentiment. Contact with the Word will save us from the danger of communicating a shallow Gospel that neither challenges nor changes a world that already believes what you have to say.

(2) Of our contact with the world I have already spoken at some length; but we have still to draw some conclusions that affect our preaching. Suppose we begin at the beginning, and ask how a real contact with the modern world will condition the background, the preparation of what we have to say.

In the first place, the shape of the sermon that is

WQ5
R22

rising in our mind will not be determined by some admired model, by some ideal conception of a masterpiece of preaching, but by our knowledge of the minds and needs of the ordinary men and women who are going to hear us. It is here that the traditional pattern of preaching can lead us astray. Most of us still are drawn to the classical conception of a sermon, with its rounded phrases, its balanced periods, its dramatic illustrations, and its logical sequence. It would be an immense loss if we ceased to read the great sermons of the past, or abandoned the Scottish tradition of careful and logical construction. But I am more and more convinced that our contact with the modern world must mean a quite different construction from that of the ages of faith and hope. If we really feel on our pulses the nervous tension and apocalyptic tempo of the present day, how can we sit down to write those calm and shapely paragraphs, and produce these neat and tidy answers?

We can learn from one who is concerned to communicate something quite different—the 'scientific attitude'. Professor Waddington writes: 'Measured utterances have disappeared from present-day use because our thought, more turbulent and contradictory, more ready to apprehend something of which it had been previously unaware, does not fit that form. Their disappearance is deeply connected with our change to a society in which the comfortably off have orange-juice before breakfast instead of family prayers.'[1] How many 'measured utterances' roll off

[1] *The Scientific Attitude*, by C. H. Waddington (Pelican).

Mission House
Seminary Library

the sermon assembly-lines week by week, and how few make any impression whatever on the target.

There are, of course, occasions when we have to be more formal and measured, but even then I believe that modern preaching must be as direct and realistic as possible. If we are truly in contact with the world to-day there will be a sympathetic tension in our words, and the 'peace of God' which lives in them will indeed be the 'peace that passeth all understanding' and not the phoney peace that comes with the familiar phrase of traditional piety. The shape of our sermons will be determined by a ruthless honesty that continually asks: 'Is this the kind of thing that I would say to Bill in this way, and would be prepared to defend it man to man?' (And a useful supplementary question is: 'Have I put in this illustration because it really lights up the difficult point I'm making, or because I can put it over with dramatic effect?') Modern preaching will surely reflect the ignorance and doubts as well as the certainties of the committed Christian. Honesty will surely limit the number of assured 'answers' we are prepared to give, and make us dissatisfied to be retailers for the rest of our lives of the solutions to difficulties we absorbed as students from our textbooks or professors.

This contact with the world in the preparation of sermons means also an effort on the intellectual level. The preacher ought to be reading the books and poems, seeing the plays and films and paintings, hearing the music of the present day to the limit of his natural capacity. This may seem obvious enough, but there would surely be more reflection in the modern pulpit of the tension and confusion revealed in the world of art if preachers were really in contact with it in a serious way—and not just to pick out this or that extravagance for sensational abuse. It is a dangerous half-truth to say that of course the Christian knows the answer that releases the tension and 'gives to wild confusion peace'. This is not the kiss of peace: it is the kiss of death. It is the attempt to avoid Gethsemane. The preacher has in every generation a debt to the artist, and to-day he should be sharing his sensitivity to the disorder of the human spirit. A by-product of this contact would be the emergence from our congregations of the genuine Christian artist, the novelist, the poet, the dramatist, the musician, who could express in their medium not only Gethsemane but Easter. There are hopeful signs that here in Scotland, and in many other countries, this development is taking place.

Contact with this world has everything to do with the preacher's use of words. For just as the Word Incarnate spoke the Aramaic idiom of His day; and just as the apostles proclaimed the message in the *Koiné* of the Middle East; so the word-pattern of our preaching must reflect the real language of to-day. I say the 'real language' for there is a pulpit jargon that passes for genuine speech, but consists of phrases, and even words, that no one but a preacher would use. If it were simply a matter of finding the most accurate formulae for imparting a series of beliefs this use of a peculiar idiom would be serious enough. But when we bear in mind that God's Word cannot be so formulated, and that modern study of the use of words tends to confirm the view that they are not simply symbols for conveying propositions but are means of personal communion and of introducing others to new areas of experience, then it becomes the more imperative to find in preaching the current terms of communication and not the traditional phraseology of the churches.

It is sometimes supposed that real contact with the modern world can be achieved by a radical process of simplification. Encouraged by the doubtful compliment, 'I *did* enjoy your children's address', many a minister has set himself to a drastic pruning of the intellectual content of his adult sermons. Where this means attempting to say less in the time available it is certainly a good discipline for most of us; but where it means the reduction of the Gospel to a thin moralism, dispensed in avuncular chatter, it is a disastrous policy. When we consider the quality of many newspaper articles and radio talks to which our generation give their attention from time to time, it is absurd to suppose that they are incapable of adult religious thinking. To communicate we must be understandable, but that does not necessitate addressing our contemporaries continually in the manner and language of the religious kindergarten.

There is one other point of contact with the modern world on which something quite categoric can be said. There may be things which cannot be expressed in the language of the street; there may even be words and phrases which the Church must retain as her own possession. But there can be no possible excuse for preaching *sounding* different from any other kind of public speech. This is not my province, but I am convinced that this question of voice and tone, which seems to many of the clergy a minor matter, is of great importance to the modern man or woman. Why should it be that when you switch on a radio-set in the middle of a programme nine times out of ten you can tell if it is a sermon that is being preached? If we are in real contact with the world, and have sensitive ears, surely we can speak of the Good News in much the same voice and accent as that in which someone else reads the ordinary news?

(3) Preaching means contact with the Word, and contact with the world, *in the context of the Church*. This last phrase is no mere religious convention. At all times preaching has been a function of the Church, and not just of an individual. Men are set apart for it— they have even set themselves apart for it—but essentially it arises out of the common life of the Church. The first Christians, after Pentecost, 'continued steadfastly in the apostles' doctrine and fellowship'. The doctrine was thus related to the fellowship, the preaching to the community. And both were related to the 'breaking of bread and prayers'. In one way or another this church-context has been determinative of Christian preaching ever since.

If we look again at the pattern of modern preaching, I think we can detect the way in which the age of individualism loosened the ties between preaching and the fellowship. The break-up of the parish community; the emergence of anonymous industrialized man; the conception of religion as 'what a man does with his solitariness'; the emphasis on the sermon as a solo performance to a group of comparative strangers— all these factors contributed to the isolation of the sermon from the living context of a congregation and parish. During the same period the theologian was at times moving far from the life of the worshipping Church, and the preacher tended to follow him along the same track. The results of this are still with us in the habit of regarding the sermon as a Sunday lecture, or 'pep-talk', proceeding solely from the individual mind and experience of the preacher; and also in the type of preaching that appears to have more connection with the latest theological or philosophical debate than with the ongoing life of the congregation as a living fellowship. Here, of course, we touch on a vicious circle in our church life: for a living fellowship needs true preaching, and there can be no true preaching without at least some element of real fellowship. The revival of preaching in our generation and the revival of church-consciousness, both local and universal, go hand in hand.

What has been called the 'rediscovery of the Church' in our time has immense significance for the preaching of the Word. It is not only that we are now increasingly aware that the preacher is not a 'wandering voice' but in a real sense a mouthpiece of the Church Universal: in a quite concrete way here and there the local church is coming alive and bringing the preacher into a real relationship with his flock. To-day there are numerous signs of such communities appearing among our churches, communities who share a common concern, and who are prepared to be the Church in action. Parish missions, action groups, visitation teams, and the like, are vigorous examples of this kind of life that is starting up in all quarters of the Christian Church to-day. And from this activity there is emerging a new and fruitful relationship between the sermon and the fellowship.

This surely is what is meant by 'the context of the Church'. It is not simply that the Church supplies the background, supports the preacher, fills the pews; but that a man called to declare the Word of God is working in close harmony with a body of men and women who are seeking truly to be the Body of Christ, His instrument for the recreation of the world —beginning where they are. It is as one of this vital fellowship that the preacher will declare the Word, and when he specifically seeks contact with the pagan world they are his information-service, his co-workers, his bridge-head. Preaching, to be effective in our world, must break with the tradition of the 'solo performer' and be constantly related to the Christian community in action.

This problem of communication which we have been considering in the sphere of preaching is a general problem affecting the whole of modern society. It may even be that upon its solution depends the fate of our civilization. For the Christian Church it has taken on a peculiar urgency, since we believe that the message we have to deliver is relevant to the whole situation of misunderstanding, isolation, and suspicion. It is our task to bend our whole energies to make that message intelligible and vital to our contemporaries. And we can have hope that, under God, it can be done. For underneath the web of words and symbols in which we seem to be entangled, God's truth and man's need communicate to-day as in the past. It is to people who need to know of some power in control of events, who need a central loyalty among the competing claims, and who need a moral dynamic by which to live, that we speak in the Name of the Father, and of the Son, and of the Holy Spirit.